LIFE

LOVE

LUST

An eclectic collection of poetry throughout life's journeys

By Kathleen Walker

"LifeLoveLust" copyright © 2009 by Kathleen Walker, all rights reserved. Reproduction without the express written consent of the author is prohibited. Thank you for respecting the authors work.

Table of Contents

Life
- A Single Grain
- Where Do Dreams Go To Die?
- The Dimmest Stars
- To Be Free
- Pretty Pills
- Boozed
- Broken Wings
- Choking My Happiness...
- Crazy Is As Crazy Does
- Depression
- I've Gone Mad! A Spiritual Journey
- Leave Me Be
- Planting Seeds
- A Sinners Prayer
- Age...In The Nude!

Love
- Brian's Song
- They're Only Words
- Childsplay
- Cosmic Love
- Drown Me Slowly
- He...His...Him
- Perseverance
- Quiet Reflections
- These Are The Times
- Torn And Tattered
- I Didn't Want To Love Him

Lust

    An Escape To Remember
    Baby, Can You Hear My Passion?
    I Woke At 5 A M
    For Lovers Only
    Skinny Dipping
    Soft Whispers
    Torture
    Veronica's Random Encounter
    As If...

Epilogue And Inspiration

    Ode To Edgar Allan Poe

Previous publication credits:

"I Woke At 5 A M" ~ Featured in "The Jimston Journal", March 2007 and placed in the top 20 of "The Secret Attic", poetry competition March 2007.

"A Single Grain" ~ Appeared in the online e-zine "The Cats Meow For Writers And Readers", September 2007.

"Drown Me Slowly" ~ Featured in the maiden issue of "The Far Side Of Midnight", January 2008.

"To Be Free" ~ Received the prestigious Editors Choice Award from "The Enchanting Verses International", Summer 2008.

LIFE

"A Single Grain"

Sand, a single grain
Inconspicuous on its own
Blown about
Alone

Has little relevance
Without a crowd
Of friends to help
Yet stands proud

Held in my hand
Singularly it falls
Blowing away in the wind
No significance at all

By the handful
Thousands of grains
Together binds
Sandcastles in the rain

All that hard work
Washed away
Our tedious efforts
Scatter where they may

A single grain
So fragile, yet so strong
Securing bricks of life
Together they belong

"Where Do Dreams Go To Die?"

Where do dreams go to die?
Is it somewhere far?
Way beyond the sky
Do they feel as sad as we?
That our hopes have vanished
How can this be?
We've lived so long
With our dreams intact
They've evaporated…too quickly gone
But now… how do we revel?
Dreams that were destined
To take us to the next level
They've died a sudden death
After years of anticipation
We collectively held our breath
Waiting for them to materialize
To get a life of their own
To take wings and fly
Where do dreams go to die?
I want to go where they go
A serene place to never again cry

"The Dimmest Stars"

On an eerie foggy night
Amidst a spray of murky, cloudy mist
Stars beam down from above the bog
An imploring, beseeching squeal
"Take note of me!"
The plea came forth from a muted one
Refusing to be ignored
Whilst the intensely bright ones constellate
In a fashioned cliquish troupe
Snubbing those who dim in contrast

The out casted…hovering in a shiver
The reverse of the looking glass remains
Forever their only course
Again, the bravest dared speak
"But I am unblemished,
Why can't I be as you?"
The most vivid responded, brusque
"You are petty and small,
Be gone! You don't belong among us!"

Collected, the dim demurely muttered
"Your arrogance is duly noted.
A momentous time will come,
Then you shall see my brilliance.
Perhaps not in lightness, I pale in your brightness,
However, my relevance will be exposed."

As is the downtrodden star,
The dim of earth are quietly strong
Abide with patience and wait
For the brighter to squeal like little piglets
To be saved from their own egos

"To Be Free"

To be free
the poem writes me

thoughts spill into print
no effort at all put into it

at times a burden on paper to bear
no control for creativity there

words roll onto the keyboard
effortlessly, waves of ideas soared

making their way to the screen
my fingers know what my thoughts mean

liken to birds ascending into their bliss
the words connect and teach me this

I cannot control it anymore than stop breathing
I pray my prose to others have meaning

for if only a few my gift does touch
even if only a few would please me much

"Pretty Pills"

all the pretty pills…
which ones do I take?
some put me to sleep
some keep me awake
I could combine them
see clouds in festive shapes
what dreams I would have
lucid visions they make
some clear my head
others strangle my thoughts
down velvet paths I've been led
hallucinogens of naught
am I seeing things for real?
or am I paranoid?
illusions make me feel
where once, I was void
and now there is no feeling at all
my body…lifeless and numb
so far from grace I do fall
not as blessed as are some
who aimlessly go through life
yet come out smelling like a rose
immune from everyday strife
heart hardened and closed
hurting others along their way
they suffer not for their evil deeds
they see it as comical play
on my pain their ego feeds
so…I will drown my sorrow
what will be…will be
I pray there be no tomorrow
oh, pretty pills... set me free

"Boozed"

There is nothing quite so fine
As a crystal glass of wine
I stood stoic to admire
A sparkling red…red as fire
Ever so elegantly I sipped
To not disturb its grapey gift
Around and around I swished and swirled
The delicate taste my tongue encurled
The finest of aroma awash
Around my schnoz it did accost
Sipping and gulping to hearts content
Swallowing down as elbow bent
The glass habitually moving to my lips
A happy dance invaded my hips
Pouring the last drops from that heavenly bottle
My mind went fuzzy, my efforts throttled
The euphoric high from those darn grapes
Had me tearing down the drapes
Adorning my nakedness in toga I fashioned
Lamp shade atop my head had me a-dancin'
O Lord! On the table I jumped
The high of the sparkling goodness had me pumped!
Then at once the room was a-spinnin'
Amid the dancin', laughter and grinnin'
I crashed to the floor, falling with great fanfare
Facedown I lay then fell asleep there
Awaking in the morn amongst all the ruins
My head ached and pounded, my lips drooled fluids
I staggered to my feet, and wobbled quite wearily
Looked around the room and muttered…oh, verily
There must have been a party here
Memory is hazy, to great fear
Surely, I must have had a good time
Me, the drapes, the lamp shade, the table and the wine

"Broken Wings"

stumbling and falling
in daily life
picking myself up
dusting myself off
holding my head high
continuing life's fateful journey
the giddy adrenaline filled high highs
and deflating bottom of the barrel low lows
smiling idiocy through it all
spreading cheer among the apathetic
at times crying alone in my bed at night
feeling forgotten and lonely
complete isolation
all the while surrounded by others
...an unexplainable, painful void
others perceive me as flaky, airhead, confused
I see me as flawed, with a big heart and good intentions
ever vigilant in my quest of happiness and well being for all
I love others in spite of flaws
why can't I be loved?
criticism and hypocrisy run rampant
there is no degree of sin
we are all earthly angels
with broken wings

"Choking My Happiness..."

Choking my happiness to death
Unspoken secrets, twisted and sick
Walking on egg shells, I hold my breath
While loathing bad habits I long to kick

The world gets in the way of seeing clearly
How can I be so cool and calm?
Happiness is close....or, perhaps very nearly
I wait nervously for the exploding bomb

To drop… as most surely it will
Life isn't so naïve as to think
I know that what is truly real
Will definitely bring me to the brink

Of breakdown…eminent and so sure
Sunshine days lending a surreal disguise
Reality becomes a deceiving blur
Serving to numb… I can only surmise

And so I will proceed…with caution
The egg shells reminding me to tread
Ever so lightly…don't dare create motion
Along my path of loneliness, sadness, and dread

"Crazy Is As Crazy Does"

crazy is as crazy does
those who don't know me may say
they think my brain doesn't work properly
that airhead, clouded thoughts get in the way
we all go off the deep end at times
some days are better than others
if I had to make a choice about how I lived
I'd say my life is my druthers
your life may seem normal to you
my life a chaotic mess
I know exactly where everything is
you just don't understand me, I guess
My brain functions normally
no cobwebs, no clouds, no dead air
I plot, plan, map out my destiny
of others opinions I choose not to care
others believe it's important what they think of me
they think I'm flaky, disheveled and scattered
dunno why they think their opinion is important
like they are someone who mattered
I answer to no one, save myself
I must be true to only me
for when I look in the mirror
me is the only person I see

"Depression"

What darkens my door?
Your existence…sinister
Creating disruption
A disturbance in my comfort zone
Lost and lonely, eternally alone

I feel you there…leering, glaring
Hollow eyes, gloomy and decrepit
A vapor…crouching, preying
A rabid bat awaiting its capture
Thieving my void skeleton for the rapture

Hanging above me
Watching, patiently biding
My anguish, my breakdown
You witness my untimely demise
Your phony cheeriness a disguise

What darkens my door?
Failure tarries, awaiting its glory
To bask in my misfortune
My unblessed existence
Danger eminent, feeble resistance

Neurosis overwhelming
Panic sets in, give in to the terror
Fear a reality of what lies
Step by step in succession
You've won again, dark depression

"I've Gone Mad! A Spiritual Journey"

Reflecting on life
Is causing great strife
To suddenly realize
What others see with their own eyes
I believe I've gone mad
Yes, mad ~ I'm bad!
How have I lived so long unaware?
Apparently some absent cells there
I must say, the ones in the brain
I've obviously misplaced them again…and again
For no one could have lived so long thus
And not been informed to be of the daft among us
I've always thought *them* to be
One of *them*…certainly not me
Was it the purple polka dot dress?
Clued them in, I must be distressed
Or perhaps it's the orange stripe hat?
It does have demure white mixed in with that
Maybe it was the short bus poetry!
Alas! That is it! That's what exposed me!
No, that's just rubbish…pure garbage
It can't be my gift of assembling the verbiage
I can only surmise it must be the eyes
Hinting of sweetness amid all the lies
"We're sailing tomorrow, will you come?"
They knew I was lying, not biting my tongue
Fear of large bodies of water baffles some
My phobia is very real, pray don't think me dumb
And, yes…as a matter of fact I do hear voices
They speak at odd times, leaving me no choices
The apparitions appear without fail
And, no!…I do not belong in a mental jail
It's a simple kind of mad, a cheerful silliness

Please refrain from portraying me a villainess
Memories of madness pepper me now
Age is relentless that way…and how!
I reflect on the many times others have said
"She's lost it, gone bonkers, crazy in the head!"

"Leave Me Be"

Please, oh please...leave me be
Everything happens in its own time
To think of more tearing away at me
Gives valid reason for my daydreaming crime

Of the ludicrous and outrageous kind
No sanity or reason is found
I fear loss of my normally sound mind
Too tightly wound, I'm anxiously bound

By out of control issues and unresolved fear
My thoughts race, my impatient heart pounds
No logic or reason, my ears fail to hear
The stress rises in disproportionate mounds

Not one more thing can my fragile psyche bare
No matter how trivial or small
Just one more thing to deal without care
A breakdown and most certain to fall

Spiraling down from a tower so tall
Gleaming shiny, admired en masse
We can't be perfect one and all
Oblivious, we live in our houses of glass

Why is it so difficult to allow one
The time much needed alone
When my thoughts of prose are done
I'll emerge from my cocooned comfort zone

Until then please patiently await
My attention to all your needs
When I am done with this obsession of fate
I'll garden your emotional weeds

"Planting Seeds"

Planting seeds
A simple task
Pull the weeds
No questions asked

We toil about
Our days oblivious
A chore, no doubt
But I *am* curious

Do we really know?
As we plant our seeds
Or do we blindly go
Tending our daily needs

Each little deed in kind
The blossoms not seen til later
Having faith will unwind and unbind
As intended by our maker

So…plant some seeds
Of goodness will grow
Let go of greed
Your kindness will show

"A Sinners Prayer"

Oh gentle spirit
Move in me
The will to abide
To truly be free

End tears that sadden
Shed fears that bind
My heart is heavy
Oh please, be kind

Awaken in me the light
Of your love
So I might feel
Your gentle hand from above

Reaching down from your throne
To touch my heart
Grant courage and strength
I've sinned from the start

I beg sweet forgiveness
Salvation from strife
My prayer for us all
Everlasting pure life

"Age ~ In The Nude!"

Age is a curious thing
Youth craves bling
Age craves comfort
A feel good thing, of sorts

Age compels me
Be as relaxed as I can be
To drink wine in the nude
Youth consider it crude

Clothing optional suits me well
No inhibitions, can't you tell?
I feel so constricted by clothes
A freedom without, heaven knows

If per chance my carefree offends you
I certainly can tell you what you should do
You must find a way to shed your cover
The way you do in the company of a lover

Project your freedom sans limits sublime
Remember you came here perfectly fine
Your birthday suit was all good and well
And in the end when you hear that bell

Ringing joyfully from heaven above
To the light you'll ascend in the warm love
No one there will say you have less class
Whether or not you've covered your ass

LOVE

"Brian's Song"

Melodic chords
Echo softly
Strings strummed
Enrapture to another world
The beauty of you that shines
Through those magical fingers
Sends chills
A trance…a dance
Of lovely melodious bliss
Calming…silky…smooth
A tiny glimpse inside, else disguised
Fragile and breakable
As a faint whisper, demure and understated
Providing a connection of heart and soul
Through a beautiful musical gift
Few others will ever know

"They're Only Words"

They're only words
"Love" "Kindness" "Caring"
When spoken
They give comfort, blindly
An illusion
That all which is done for concern
Of another's well being
Really matters. It does not.

Because they're only words
They roll off the tongue. Smooth as silk
Bestowing warm fuzzies and goose bumps
Giving false sense of reassurance
Of love
Where none exists
Disengenuine, fodder intended to rob the soul

They're only words
Lending insincere hope
And giving artificial calm
To those in need
Whose esteem is lowered to the bowels of hell
Instilling a belief that
Emotions are relevant. They are not.

"Childsplay"

like children we play

these games we play

ne'er a mind given

while carelessly livin'

not a whim or care

for sorrow borne there

nor selfish love taken

for passion we're makin'

beguiled we've lost

those lovers we've tossed

one could be the one

lone, would we have known...

with blinders we wander

forsaken fields yonder

"Cosmic Love"

Cosmic energy
Transforms fear into love
As satin ribbons of moonlight
Constellate
Mystical and hypnotizing
Begging acquiescence
Reticence morphs into
Acceptance
A beautiful dance
Of intertwining souls
Meshed, as a single being
Encompassing
Resistance is futile
Surrender eminent
Complete and unconditional
Fusion
Of two hearts
Beating as one
Breathless and wanton
United

"Drown Me Slowly"

Drown me slowly
So I can look into your eyes
while you push me under
as I see your face

Drown me slowly
so I can hold onto your strong hands
my shattered heart slows beating
the water engulfing me
as I grip your wrists to feel your pulse

Drown me slowly
so I can relive our passion together
sweet memories rush through my head
the once tender times we had
as I reach out for your touch

Drown me slowly
so I can beg not to live
in a world without your love
no more to feel the warmth of your body
as I pray forgiveness for my sins

Drown me slowly
so I can forget I already feel dead inside
never again to kiss your lips
please remember my unending love for you
as I gasp my last breath

Drown me slowly…

"He... His...Him "

He has no room in his heart
for anyone, leave him
he is unaware of his unawareness
he cannot recognize himself in prose

I speak to you, my darling
unleash your inner passion
outwardly stoic is so upper crust
smugly refusing penetration of emotion

Oh... it is there
I've seen a semblance of it
it's been expended on canvas
...canvas oblivious to your pain

The canvas absorbs every ounce of your emotional energy
thirsting for the attention you labor on it with brush and color
not with rejection, but artificial affection
complete unconditional acceptance

You use it and abuse it in a wanton manner
making love to it through graceful deliberate strokes of a fine brush
with lust women would cherish to have thrust upon them
orgyesque... reckless and savage

Though you settle
for satisfying emotionless physical pleasure
void of feeling the joy
two bodies know melding breathlessly into one being

No worries, my darling
we will meet again, our souls reunited

forever linked by chance happenstance
purpose and perfect circumstance

But for now, physically brought together
a rush of adrenaline waxes memory of eyes connecting
counterclockwise motion of time
begs to try our patience

"Perseverance"

the sun sets
As the day winds down
Dinner bakes in the oven
Sips of wine aid stresses of the work day subside…slowly
Household activity bustling, rattling, the clanging of sauce pans
Small talk. And chatter…the usual daily queries
"How are the kids?"
I talk to your back as you walk away without waiting for my response
I persevere for a connection
You pop the top of your beer with a *whoosh*…
And 18 wheelers on the big screen take precedence over conversation
"How was your day?" Routine, uninterested…but at least you ask
"Hectic…busy…swamped with phone calls and demands"
Not waiting for my answer, you blast the big rigs
While I express my frustrations of the day
You…oblivious to my words
Snacking on crackers and cheese, you return to your distraction on the screen
I continue dinner preparations, going through the motions of happiness…
Silently, I persevere for comfort through food
As if contentment would return based upon that
"The way to a mans heart, is through his stomach"
I remember my conservative mother preaching
Her urgings engrained in my psyche. Not discouraged, I persevere
While from the 42" plasma screen
The earth movers blare in the foreground of my life
I realize, in an epiphany, this *IS* my life
Mundane, ordinary, anticlimactic
"Is dinner ready yet?"
With heavy sigh, realizing this pathetic stimulus is all that will be

"Almost" I mutter, with another sip of my wine
While eagles fly over mountains on the Discovery channel
And I dream of far away places with carefree laughter and
frivolity
There should be more
I want more
Somewhere, there must be more…
I persevere to find it

"Quiet Reflections"

How did I get to this place in life
quiet reflection being what it is...nonexistent

overcast days of winter loom perilously
over the darkness that is my soul

reason and sanity have escaped
where once they abided proudly

the vampire that you are drained me completely
of the life blood that once pumped hope and vigor to my brain

slaying those pesky breakup dragons
can be so exhausting

re-landscaping to kill the weeds that grew while we tried to cultivate
our failed relationship can be such a laborious chore

so... if you need to do a little grass burning to soothe your soul....
go for it, baby...whatever gets you through...

"These Are The Times..."

these are the times I sit and cry
while better times pass me by
I want to be happy, I really try
I want to stop living the lie
I feel my spirit fly
take off into the sky
I can feel my insides die
can't figure out why
you chose to ditch me on the sly
tearful, sad good bye
no more feeling the high
of what togetherness did imply
loss of closeness we can't deny
labored breathing with a sigh
I thought you'd always be nearby
now I'm left alone, no dry eye
these are the times I sit and cry...

"Torn and Tattered "

Here I sit broken hearted
Tried to move on
Tears have started
Can't say anything cute
Been aching since we parted
A burden to my ego
Has me feeling martyred
No relief from the sad goodbye
I should be drawn and quartered
My instincts were clear
A warning that I wouldn't matter
In your life I've become the former
Just another one of the latter
You said I could be the lucky one
Yes, I do remember that banter
Was it simply smoke and mirrors
Or plumping the lie fatter
I am hurt and angry
By the moment, getting madder
For being taken in, not once but twice
The humiliation is making me sadder
Hopeless despair rings in my head
Broken heart torn and tattered

"I Didn't Want To Love Him"

I didn't want to love him. I wanted to be his friend. He was grateful for friendship. We talked of small things. Weather and music and...whatnot. Of how daunting life can be. The everyday trivial turning to crisis. A struggle at every corner. He frequently made promises I knew he couldn't keep. I kept my expectations low. Less probability of disappointment that way. But he made a promise to be there for me, and...he was there. Waiting patiently for a first glimpse. Our eyes met with hello! And big hugs...and instantly I knew I didn't want to love him

His eyes appeared in a sleepy dream I'd had. In the form of a lost, forlorn puppy. I picked him up and held him close. I took him home with me and warmed him and fed him. He nuzzled my neck and gave me slobbery kisses...and instantly I knew I didn't want to love him.

Because I knew he would break my heart. But those sad puppy dog eyes had a grip on me I couldn't unleash. His overwhelming desire to be loved, an unconditional acceptance he hadn't known. And I gave it to him with all my heart and soul. Encompassing, mad and passionate. Just as I succumbed, he had to move on. He thanked me for my kindness, then vanished in the dark of night. Leaving me with empty arms, an empty bed, and an emptier heart. Still, I'm a better woman for having known him. Some days I reflect and remember him fondly. And recall the magic of those eyes and the time when ...instantly I knew I didn't want to love him.

LUST

"An Escape To Remember "

Winged euphoria
floated above our intertwined bodies
looking down on us
mimicking angels keeping watch

Time reversed itself
for an escape to remember
frozen, etched, tangible
it reached out to capture our ecstasy

Once was not enough
to know if our euphoria
would endure the inevitable
of time moving forward

An escape to remember
must be forever known
as only a memory now
our bodies never to be together again

Euphoria escaped our grip
as we tried to hold on
to something non-existent
only imagined in a hazy dream

"Baby, Can You Hear My Passion?"

Blindly searching for truths that don't tell lies
I feel myself doubting it all
Are we even honest with ourselves in our dreams?
So far from grace, oh…how far we fall
I find myself in second place as your number one
Or, is it in first place as your second choice?
Taking a backseat to another so close
To you…and I have no audible voice
To shout it from the roof tops
Oh… how I wish I could
Must be silent, must be still
Staying under wraps is good
Sweet dreams, my darling
I hope you're sleeping well
So far away under starry skies
Where dreamy moonlight heroes dwell
Do my words reach you at all?
Or are they merely noise in the air
Is there any penetration of emotion?
From my passion so obviously there
I wish words could express
The depth of my love for you
It is you I am voracious to completely devour
Oh…the sensuous things I long to do
The stirrings within are a richness
Incomparable to anything I've ever known
Can't you feel my unwavering passion?
My craving for you has grown
Can you hear my faint whispers?
Softly crooning…*"I want you so bad"*
Can't think clearly at all
This desire is driving me completely mad
I've tried drowning my want in alcohol

And writing about it without fail
To tell how much I need your touch
I fear this stranded ship may never sail
What a waste it would be
To toss away such desire and lust
Sexual energy we can't deny
Alas... Staying apart we must
Although I have your passion
Another has claimed your heart
I will never completely have you
It's not just the miles that keep us apart
My heart aches beyond belief...
Unrealistic... my obsession with you...

"I Woke At Five AM"

I woke at five AM
The smell of your perfume filled my head
Craving the touch of your soft skin
But when I reached out to touch you
You were not in my bed
A lonely vision filled with desire
I longed to hold you close
To feel your soft breathing on my neck
Erotic whispers and the euphoric high
Of your lips on mine fuels the fire
Of want and lustful passion I hold
Here in my heart
Your lack of presence leaves a void
Wider than the Grand Canyon
And we are miles apart
The ache to have you near is unbearable
The pain, stabbing and sharp
I woke at five AM
The smell of your perfume filled my head
I drank a gallon of coffee to rid myself
Of the emptiness I felt
Not having you here is torture for sure
But that scent fills the air and
I can see your face so clear
Sometimes life is cruel and unfair
Like when you wake at five AM
Thirsty like the desert to feel bodies embrace
And the one you want…isn't there

"For Lovers Only "

The flowers are beautiful, my dear
The candy... oh so sweet
The love letter you wrote to me
Makes this festive day complete

Together we'll savor steak with red wine
Gaze longingly into each others eyes
Illuminated with the dim glow of candlelight
You know I love your sweet surprise

To show how much you love me
No other words need to be said
Your deep affection moves me passionately
Yet...I know, you really just wanna get laid!

"Skinny Dipping"

Shimmering pools of vibrant blue
I could skinny dip in your eyes
Oh, the lusty fantasies of you
One glance…one wink…my darling, tell me some lies

Virtual touch grazing along silken skin
Inviting your lust, shamelessly beckoning
Erotic thoughts wrought with sin
Open the door to redemption and reckoning

Any semblance of sanity escapes without care
Your warmth of desire a primary mission
Hungry bodies sweating droplets do dare
Boldly pumping in rhythm, together we glisten

Sweet slumber conjures dreams of such
Deep within those vibrant blue pools
The mirage of you escapes my clutch
Wicked dreams play tricks and fool

"Soft Whispers"

Soft whispers with shallow breathing
sensual movement of bodies flowing freely
together as one, melted in passion
a vision of unity as never before
soft whispers arouse
a high not achieved with any drug
intoxication in its purest form
finer wine could not match the euphoria
soft whispers as your lips meet mine
in a magic kiss our mouths embrace
fireworks shoot into the still night
illuminating the dark sky intertwined with the glowing stars
soft whispers echo in my ears
with erotic grace and rhythm
tingling, twitching, gasping with pleasure
beyond belief...you take my breath away

"Torture"

You stand so proud
Belittling out loud
Crooked finger the accuser
At me…you say *I'M* the loser
Your high horse parades
But your arrogance will fade
Your snide smirks glancing
Wild, frenzied eyes dancing
Not one more time can I take
Not one more appearance can I fake
Not one more put down from you
Those days behind me…you will rue
I have you by the balls
Your squeaky voice calls
Mercy screams, to no avail
This time, *YOU* fail
I planned my revenge with care
While you're tied down over there
With my shiny razor sharp blade
Precision cuts are made
Around the sack, a perfect slice
You're screaming in pain…sinfully nice
The agony you've caused me returned to you now
Your faint pleas ask me…why? How?
How could I inflict such horror?
You twitch…I revel…how much more?
Inserting the blade below your dick
Blood squirts projectile with each prick
For every time you punished me…
Every time you made me feel to be
Small, irrelevant, like I was worthless
You're the one, petty and aimless
Take care, my dear

I no longer fear
A beating or a threat
I give what you get
You suffer…your blood in a pool
Eyes begging…make you the fool
The tables are turned
A woman spurned
I carefully dismember your sensitive part
With skilled precision…an artists art
Die peacefully, darling...although you deserve naught
My torture, your torture, we're even…your soul must rot

"Veronica's Random Encounter"

How does one express the loneliness?
Feeling isolated…an eerie still
How to decipher the mental mess?
That which silently schemes to break my will

The random encounters serve to appease
A temporary relief of isolation fix
Succumbing…surrendering with shameless ease
Impossible to resist those beckoning lips

My darling, I crave your fiery passion
Another with ties to you strives to keep us apart
My will to have you in any fashion
Eyes meet, emitting sparks from the start

Another with claims to your desirous frame
Pleads with me to take flight and vacate
I have no intention to separate, nor her to maim
But simply to have you without wait

The heat of our bodies melds together…effortlessly
She waits at home…paces, worries, frets
Her eyes teary with pain and cannot see
She lost you long ago…her commitment she now regrets

Although she didn't lose you to me
Lovers have yet to be revealed…nonetheless so
Your lust for another would passionately be
An irresistible, unparalleled rush you well know

Your arms around me steals reality away
Your eager lips take me to another world
Together our bodies rhythmically sway

I giggle and twitch…our legs illicitly curled

Impossible to escape the euphoria and high
An addiction...no adequate words can say
I fear destruction of self is nigh
A passionate death I dream of …No!… I crave…

"As If..."

Miraculously, my lungs continue to breathe

breath after breath, in and out

my chest moves with each gasp

still…my eyes blink

the sandy saltiness

begs to be flushed away

my thoughts continue

to weave…uncontrollable

my mouth salivates at the thought

of your lips on mine

my legs long to intertwine with yours

my arms reach out for you

though you're not there

and you won't be...

my heart and soul know your absence

yet my physical being continues to function

...as if there were a reason to live

EPILOGUE

&

INSPIRATION

"Edgar Allan Poe"

How I love reading Poe!
His twisted thoughts painfully so
Thought provoking and strange
No chatter of home on the range
So cleverly he rhymed
Each stanza perfectly timed
Sorrow abounds, no holds barred
Recanting how brutally his heart was scarred
How he missed his beloved so much
Abandoned him...stranded, left in the clutch
Of sadness...heartbroken and down
Only one thing could reverse his frown
One little dose of happiness so pure
An elixir of ecstasy would for sure
Be his savior, his mainstay, his safety net
A little bit of magic to cure the regret
Then a little became more and more...
He needed more than ever before
Words ran together, rambling amid ruins
But poetic genius still penned fluid
No matter how little or how much
The words effortlessly flowed together as such
Thrilling delight, a vision of adoration
Just a little more...more in moderation
Of the magic potion that cures all that ails
Enabling him to write more enthralling tales
I love to hear all about sweet Lenore
Please, Edgar...please...tell me more!
And then there's the raven so hauntingly queer
Instilling its terror, dread and fear
Oh...those tales so beguiling and haughty
With a hint of an apparition and naughty
Those wonderful tales will live beyond all of our dreams

Middle of the night woes with fear and silent screams
Visions amid grand hallucinogenic trips
That fine white powder held Ed in its grip

Made in the USA
Middletown, DE
28 October 2022